HOLYHEAD' |T

For K C Saunders Esq.
Best Wishes.

Norman Jones 26·02·02

HOLYHEAD'S ROYAL VISIT

QUEEN VICTORIA'S
RETURN FROM HER LAST JOURNEY TO IRELAND

Holyhead Station, and Hotel. April 1900: A warm, pleasant day, with the sash windows raised and the curtains blowing in the cooling breeze. The photographs of the Queen's guard of honour, thought to be a Volunteer Battalion from The Welsh Regiment marching down the station approach illustrated on Pages 16 and 17 and led by their band, with flags carried at the head of the procession were taken from the vantage point of one of the windows of this hotel.

BY

NORMAN JONES · TONY ROBINSON · CAROLYN CARR

(Below) Her Majesty Queen Victoria *(seen just right of centre)* before the assembled ranks of her guard of honour and officers on the bridge of the Royal Yacht Victoria and Albert II, attended by her Ladies in Waiting is wheeled by her Indian servant on to the gang-plank (brow in naval parlance) bridging the gap between the yacht and pier. Her Majesty will then pass through the ranks of the men of the Rifle Volunteers of 2 Welsh Battalion and join the royal train waiting in the adjacent platform.

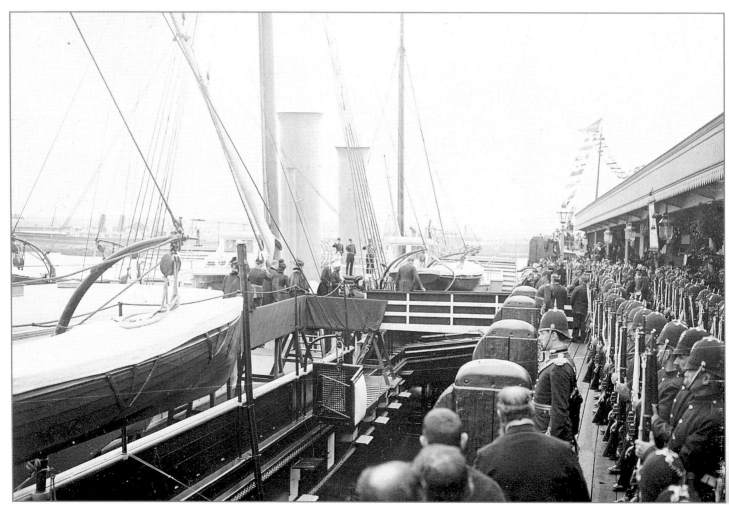

HOLYHEAD'S ROYAL VISIT

Holyhead. The Harbour of Refuge. April 1900. Salt Island divided the New Harbour from the Old and Inner Harbours, which lay to the south, the entrance to the Old Harbour being eastward of the Admiralty Pier on which stood the old Lighthouse. The Royal Yacht Victoria and Albert II makes a fine sight, paddling energetically across the harbour. In the original of this excellent picture it is just possible to distinguish the motif on the Royal Standard, whilst the Union flag streams valiantly, as does the prestigious White Ensign above the creamy wake.

INTRODUCTION

Seeing pictures of Queen Victoria being wheeled around by an Indian attendant it might be thought that her powers were failing. On the contrary despite her lack of mobility this 81 year old Royal lady in the spring of 1900 was enjoying her return to popularity immensely, and was looking forward with enthusiasm to a holiday in Ireland which she said was "entirely her own idea."

Late on the evening of Monday 2 April 1900 the L&NWR, royal train left Windsor (GW and LSW) carrying Queen Victoria and her considerable retinue on an overnight trip to Holyhead. Here next day the Queen would board her favourite and beloved royal yacht, the Victoria and Albert II on the occasion of a visit to Ireland. Victoria's last trip to that country had been a State visit in 1861. A royal train journey was the cause of mingled emotions of pride and anxiety for the railway officials and staff along the entire length of the route. The Queen once expressed the sentiment that all passenger traffic should be worked under similar rules to those relating to her journeys, a state of affairs that would have brought Britain's railway system to a permanent halt. On the appointed day the line to be traversed by the royal train was watched throughout its length. All facing points and crossing gates were locked, and each was guarded by a platelayer equipped with flags and detonators for use in the event of emergency signals being required. Traffic was to be stopped on adjacent lines whatever their direction of travel until the royal party had gone by. Emission of smoke and lifting safety valves on locomotives were prohibited and officials on the halted trains were to ensure that everything on their train was in order for the passage of the royal special. Where possible freight trains were shunted into sidings or relief roads to be clear of the running lines and wagons were to be meticulously checked to obviate the danger of overhanging or projecting loads. ....*Continued on page 5*

(Left) **Holyhead. Approach to the Admiralty Pier. April 1900:** The stock of the royal train is being moved by one of the small 'Ramsbottom' tank engines round the track of the sharp check-railed curve adjacent to the Custom House and Harbour Office which led to the Mail Pier station where Queen Victoria was to disembark from the royal yacht. Holyhead had not attained its eminence as a port without a struggle. William Arthur Maddocks MP (1773 - 1828) built his famous causeway 'The Cob' to bring the stage coaches to his new purpose built village of Tremadog intended as a last staging point for the coaches before they crossed the Lleyn Peninsula to reach the small harbour of Porth Dinllaen which Maddocks, who despite his English sounding name was born at Llandwrdnod in Denbighshire wished to develop as a major port, but the proponents of the claims of Holyhead prevailed in the Parliamentary battle.

The Royal Saloon standing in the 'Mail Pier' station: The ramp down which the Queen was to be wheeled extreme left. Roof pillars are garlanded with displays of greenery, flags and bunting. The interior dimensions of the compartments accounted for 57ft 7ins of the 60ft length of the vehicle, which could be entered by any of the three doors on each side which, although opposite to each other were not equidistant along the length of the body. The first door was situated in the dresser's compartment at the end next to the Queen's night saloon. The next gave directly onto the day saloon and is just 'off-centre' in this picture. This saloon was sumptuously furnished with a sofa and easy chairs. The third door was nearer to the end of the vehicle in the sergeant footman's compartment, occupied until his death in 1883 by Mr John Brown, and later by Abdul Karim, appointed Her Majesty's servant on 23 June 1887, his official appointment as Queen Victoria's Munshi (or clerk) being in 1889.

Holyhead, Admiralty Pier April 1900: City of Dublin Steam Packet Co., steamer. This company held the mail contract from 1849 until 1920 when it passed to the L&NWR and following the Railways Act of 1921 to the London Midland & Scottish Railway's shipping division.

Continued from page 3.......................

A pilot engine ran a few sections ahead of the royal special. Between the passing of this engine and that of the royal train, often driven personally by the Locomotive Superintendent of the particular line concerned or one of his senior assistants there was a state of breathless anticipation until the royal special passed from the section. All bridges, both over and underline would be examined and a permanent way man, or men would keep watch underneath.. Policemen stood on overline bridges to prevent any person or vehicle from crossing until the royal train had gone by. Tunnels were an especial source of worry and were rigorously patrolled. Every stationmaster was to be on duty, together with his staff as far as their duties permitted, (otherwise usually marshalled standing to attention on the platform). All signal boxes were to be manned. "Special Notices" would be issued to all staff and signalmen and the royal train signalled from box to box by its own special code. Double block working was in operation. On this occasion the train took the Great Western route to Wolverhampton, and then went by L&NWR metals to Crewe, and Chester for a stop at Llandudno Junction arrival being at 3.45am. The purpose of the overnight journey was to enable the royal party to enjoy a daylight crossing to Kingstown. At 7.45am Her Majesty's train, probably made up to 14 vehicles including the royal saloon set off again passing beneath the historic walls of Conway Castle to cross the Britannia Bridge onto Anglesey finally arriving at the Admiralty Pier, Holyhead at 9.00 a.m.

From ancient times hardy mariners had essayed the passage of the wild Irish Sea between the windswept hamlet of Holyhead with its huddle of low grey-stone buildings situated on Holy Island off the north-west tip of the Isle of Anglesey. Holyhead Mountain is only 709ft high its north-western flanks fall to the sea in steep cliffs, and at their western and northern extremities end in two rocky islets, South Stack and North Stack.

Holyhead. Shunting the Twelve-wheeled Royal Saloon: The Royal Lady disliked modernity and there was no corridor connection throughout. In 1861, Richard Bore built for the Queen at Saltley a four-wheeled saloon complete with dressing room and lavatory; the livery was claret below the waistline and white panels above. In 1869 the four-wheeler was replaced by a pair of six-wheelers, again designed by Richard Bore but built at Wolverton Works - these were the first British carriages joined by a form of flexible gangway. In 1895 the two bodies were removed from their six-wheeled chassis and united on a single frame to make the long, twelve-wheel carriage, 60ft over the headstocks illustrated here. Electric lighting was installed but the Queen insisted on the retention and use of the familiar old fashioned oil lamps in the roof and for reading preferred to use candle lamps.

(Left) Royal Saloon. The interior. April 1900: In the coach, 8ft wide over the headstocks the end lavatory/wash basin compartment was 2ft 6ins long, followed by the dresser's 13ft 5in long, leading into the royal night saloon, of 12ft 10in, and giving access to another larger lavatory/wash basin compartment 4ft 8ins long, followed by the royal day saloon 14ft 6ins; at the end of this domain yet another door led to the sergeant/footman's 'den' 7ft 0in long which contained tea and coffee making equipment, a final end cubicle arranged as another lavatory/wash basin unit was 2ft 8ins in length. The floors were double and the intervening space was cork filled, whilst the carpets were thick and luxurious. The picture shows clearly the quilted silk with which the walls and ceilings were lined, the roof structure was double whilst the interior trimming was carried out in red, white and blue watered silk. A bell push for summoning an attendant or Lady in Waiting is observed on the jamb of the right-hand side of the door frame.

(Above) Holyhead, April 1900: Viewed from the Pelham Quay, the pier is seen at low water. Holyhead Harbour, the terminus of first the road, and later also the railway from London, and the traditional departure point for Dublin and Ireland was rebuilt from 1810 onwards by John Rennie, and the Admiralty Pier, elegant Custom House and Harbour Office observed here date from this period. T. Harrison however was responsible for the Memorial Arch *(right)* on the pier; it was built in 1824 to commemorate the visit of George IV to Holyhead, when he took passage for Dun Laoghaire *(renamed Kingstown in his honour)*. The king sailed on the Thames built Post Office packet PS Lightning, 205 tons commanded by Captain Skinner the commodore captain of Holyhead. The captain, who had served in the Royal Navy was highly regarded by King George IV who gave permission for the Lightning to be renamed Royal Sovereign following his visit. Still in command at the age of 70, Captain Skinner was washed overboard and lost at sea in October 1832 from the vessel Escape. An obelisk to the captain's memory was erected overlooking the inner harbour on the east side, and served furthermore as a navigational mark, being shown in 'Charts for Coastal Navigation' (1961) as being *"in line with the Jetty Light'.*

ADMIRALTY
PIER

Holyhead, Saturday 5 August 1995: So far as the fabric of the structures the passage of almost a century seems to have wrought little change, but more indicative of modern times even than the presence of a modern Ro-Ro ferry and the green painted Gwynedd Shipping Co., Ltd., container truck, is the proliferation of razor wire, security fencing and the other preventive devices necessary to protect the port installations and members of the public from harm, which feature so prominently in this scene.   *A J Robinson*

In October 1572 during the reign of Queen Elizabeth I postal stages were set up to maintain a weekly mail service between the Court and Lord Lieutenant of Ireland, but journeying via Chester and with Liverpool as the embarkation point. Another route was via Reading, Bristol, Swansea and Milford, with a crossing to Waterford, but this was later re-routed to take advantage of the shorter sea crossing from Holyhead. At that time the port had a very poor reputation. Vessels wishing to enter the harbour (which dried out at low tide) might beat about outside for an indeterminate time waiting for a favourable westerly. Conversely other craft could be locked in the harbour by adverse conditions. The practice of the small sailing packets was to anchor off Parry's Island *(or Ynys Rug)*. On the Irish side having initially moored off Ringsend, from 1796 they used the new Pigeon House Dock in the mouth of the River Liffey. In 1810 an Act for improvements to Holyhead led to the construction of Holyhead's still extant 'Admiralty Pier' and a new harbour at Howth north east of Dublin. In 1817 Dun Laoghaire harbour was constructed, and renamed Kingstown following a visit from King George IV, still commemorated by a magnificent arch on the approach to the Admiralty Pier at Holyhead. Steamers of the New Steam Packet Company were working out of Holyhead as early as 1819, when there were seven 'official' sailing packets on the Holyhead mail service. In the late 1700's seamen on the mail packets were granted immunity from enforcement by the Press Gangs.

The road from the capital to Holyhead administered by twenty-three separate Turnpike Trusts was in atrocious condition, and in 1810 the Government commissioned Thomas Telford the noted Scottish engineer to survey the road from end to end. A new Holyhead Road, now the A5 was completed at a cost of three quarters of a million sterling. The Chester & Holyhead Railway Act of 1844 received Royal Assent on 4 July 1844 (7-8 Vic cap lxv) and empowered the promoters to raise £2,100,000 in £50 shares. The negotiations by means of which the L&NWR eventually gained control of the Chester & Holyhead railway and the cross-channel steamers were complicated, ofttimes acrimonious and lengthy. They are not relevant to these opening paragraphs setting the scene for the relationship of the British crown and particularly the Royal family and Queen Victoria with the rail and sea connections between London, Holyhead and Ireland.

The track was ready for the first train to cross the Britannia Tubular Bridge spanning the Menai Strait at 6.30am on 5 March 1850. So delighted were they with their new bridge that the next morning the directors petitioned Queen Victoria for the Prince of Wales to formally open the bridge, but as the prince was no more than 9 years of age the proposition was not entertained. Nevertheless on 13 October 1852, whilst visiting Bangor with the royal children and her beloved Prince Albert the entire royal party went via the Menai Suspension Bridge to join a royal saloon on the railway at Llanfair P.G. on Anglesey This vehicle was taken to the Anglesey end of the tube when the Queen dismounted and walked part way into the tube. Her Majesty then entered a carriage which was drawn through the tube by workmen. Prince Albert and the Prince of Wales walked over the tube accompanied by Mr Robert Stephenson who afterwards took the party down onto the shore to view the underside of the bridge.

The Royal Family were in Holyhead again in September 1853 on the occasion of a visit to Ireland. They took the opportunity to view the improvements to the facilities, conducted on their tour by James Meadows Rendel, an authority on harbour works, and one of the contractors from Messrs. Rigby's of London. They also inspected the adjacent quarries where a spectacular blast was arranged for their benefit. Stone was blasted from the slopes of Holyhead Mountain in lots of no less than 50,000 tons at a time. The material was then loaded onto large iron tip wagons on the broad gauge railway and trundled along the breakwater to the tipping site. At the time of this royal inspection the harbour improvement construction known as 'The Great Breakwater' had extended over 4,000ft into the bay. In September 1857 it had reached out to 7,000ft, 6 million tons of stone had been tipped and 1,200ft of superstructure built up to the level of high water springs.

Captain Harrison the commander of Brunel's legendary Great Eastern steamship (18,915 gt, 689ft x 82.8ft, powered by steam engines driving paddles, a single screw and also having six masts and 54,900 sq ft of sail area) together with officials of the Great Eastern Company visited Holyhead in June 1857 to discover whether the new harbour could be used as the departure point for their first transatlantic crossing. Holyhead was eminently suitable but following the many problems which beset this huge vessel, so splendidly conceived but so in advance of her time and technology, she did not arrive from Weymouth until October 1859. This was too

HOLYHEAD

A uniformed railwayman, possibly the station foreman or a traffic inspector watches intently as the stock of the Royal Train is drawn by former Ramsbottom built, open footplate 0-4-0 saddle tank locomotives from the main station towards the Admiralty Pier station. These small and light engines were used to work the stock onto and off the Admiralty Pier lines and had 14 x 20 in cylinders, 4 ft diameter coupled wheels and 120 lb per sq. in. pressure. Being designed for shunting they were fitted with lever reverse instead of the Ramsbottom screw gear for quickness of adjustment.

late for an Atlantic crossing, and she returned to Southampton to winter. Nevertheless the Great Eastern party were warmly welcomed and entertained at the Royal Hotel by the LNWR directors. Crowds occupied all vantage points to see the great ship and fifteen packed excursion trains arrived in just one day. The Royal Family were also in Holyhead at this time and Prince Albert and his guest the French Prince Napoleon were amongst the notabilities who inspected Brunel's magnificent vessel. The Great Eastern's maiden voyage Southampton - New York was on 17 June 1860, but she was not a success and the Great Ship Company went into liquidation in December 1863.

Following the death of Prince Albert on 14 December 1861 grief stricken by her loss Queen Victoria made few public appearances. When Holyhead New Harbour was completed and on Saturday 16 August 1873 a squadron of Ironclads (battleships) arrived at Holyhead for the opening ceremony with dignitaries and officials aboard, it was the Prince of Wales and the Duke of

Edinburgh who arrived on the Royal Yacht the following Tuesday. The Prince and the Duke (Prince Alfred, Ernest) travelled on the quarry railway - behind or perhaps aboard ? - one of the broad gauge 0-4-0 well tanks with 3ft 2in diameter wheels and 10in x 18in cylinders built by R. B. Longridge & Co., of Bedlington in 1852. The engine named Prince Albert for the occasion, carried them to the breakwater head where they declared the 'Harbour of Refuge' officially open. As the Queen emerged from her long period of mourning and undertook more public engagements, her popularity increased, her stature enhanced by the recovery of the Prince of Wales (later Edward VII) from typhoid and her own survival from at least one assassination attempt. There was renewed royal interest in the navy, which had lapsed in the early years following the Prince Consort's death. Interest in maritime matters and visits to dockyards and naval establishments began again, and there was a strong tradition that male members of the 'Royals' should serve in the Royal Navy.

Holyhead April 1900: The station approach, entrance and L&NWR Hotel, now demolished, and replaced by a modern building is flanked by the covered platforms. This was the occasion of Queen Victoria's passage through the port on her last visit to Ireland and a bluejacket hurries by on official business. Until 1907 there was no issue of ready made uniforms, the men merely being given an allowance of cloth to have made up, or tailor themselves.

Royal yachts have a long history. King Charles II, who returned from exile and landed at Dover 26 May 1660, had sailed from Breda to Rotterdam in a splendidly equipped yacht with decorated and gilded cabins, in fact the king so liked this ship and so extolled its good qualities that the Burgomaster of Amsterdam presented him with a similar vessel. Called the Mary she was the first in a long line of royal yachts, indeed the word is of Dutch origin, meaning a hunting or pursuit vessel - a swift ship - from jacht a hunt. King Charles is said to have designed himself a second yacht of 25 tons which he named Jamie. The Royal Sovereign of 1804 was the main royal yacht throughout William IV's reign. Victoria the niece of the bluff, hearty 'Sailor King' as he was known inherited some of his love of the sea but was not impressed with the sail-

ing yacht Royal George of 1817 *(built for George IV when he was still Prince Regent)* that she inherited, indeed Queen Victoria only used the vessel once in August 1842 on a trip to Scotland, when it was towed by two small steamers. Royal George was declared to be too slow but nevertheless remained in service as an accommodation ship for crews of other of the royal yachts until 1901.

THE ROYAL YACHTS BUILT DURING QUEEN VICTORIA'S REIGN.

1. *Victoria and Albert I.* Paddle Steamer. Launched on 26 April 1843 she was diagonally built of Danzig oak and Italian larch.

2. *Fairy* iron screw steamer launched 1845.300 tons

3. *Elfin* 98 tons the Milk Boat commissioned 1849. Paddle Steamer.

4. *Victoria and Albert II* 300 ft long. 2,470 gt. Paddle Steamer.1855

5. *Alberta* 160ft x 20ft 370 gt. Paddle Steamer.1863 To carry guests between Portsmouth and Cowes.

6. *Osborne II* launched 1868, 1,850 gt. Paddle Steamer. Used mainly by the Prince & Princess of Wales.

7. *Victoria and Albert III* 380ft x 40ft, 4,700 tons launched 1899. Screw Steamer.

On Tuesday 3rd April 1900, Queen Victoria and her retinue joined the Victoria and Albert II at Holyhead for a visit to Ireland from whence she returned on the 26th of the month. The new, larger and faster ocean going yacht Victoria and Albert III was not favoured by Her Majesty.

The Queen had intended to take a Continental holiday that year but there had been criticisms of Britain's role in the 'Boer' War from that quarter. Furthermore relations across St George's Channel had been strained, since the incident when, in the early days of her mourning the death of Prince Albert, the Queen had a statue of her late Consort carefully packed and consigned to Dublin, only to have it returned to Windsor by the Mayor and Corporation of Dublin who refused to accept it. Further souring the atmosphere, there had been no official congratulations from the same gentlemen during the acclaimed days of the Jubilee celebrations.

However reports on the gallantry of Irish troops in the South African War had healed the breach and the Queen was braving the rigours of the Irish sea to thank the Irish people personally for their support. Her Majesty had issued an instruction that on St Patrick's Day all troops 'in Her Majesty's Irish regiments' shall wear a sprig of shamrock in their head-dress'. Furthermore Victoria created a battalion of Irish Guards, the news not to be made public until she reached Dublin. The Queen liked 'pleasant surprises.'

The crossing was the reverse of smooth. The sea-sick Queen of a seafaring nation was confined to her cabin with mal-de-mer as were many of her party. Nevertheless the routine of the galley supervised by a Swiss Chef continued unabated. Multi - course meals were prepared and brought to the table, only to be consigned - untasted - to the waves. A moderate speed had been maintained by the royal yacht in accord with the adverse weather conditions, and also so that the Royal party would arrive at their destination at the time appointed for the official reception. As the storm increased in severity such ideas were abandoned, speed was increased and the yacht sailed into the safety of Kingstown Harbour long before she was due and landed her party at the Victoria Wharf at 11.30am on April 4. They were greeted by a rather breathless group headed by Lord & Lady Cadogan, who had *'put their best foot forward'* on learning of the unexpectedly early arrival of the Royal party. Eventually, when all the formalities of greeting had been complied with there commenced a 2½ hour state journey of four carriages (the Queen being the last in line) bound for the Viceregal Lodge, Phoenix Park. The King's Dragoon Guards were in attendance; the route was crowded with sailors lining part of the way, and later a Sovereign's escort of Life Guards joined the show. There was a ceremony involving the Lord Mayor of Dublin and the city keys. By this time as we know the Queen made much use of her wheelchair and as there was no lift in the Viceregal residence Queen Victoria was 'rolled a good way to the staircase' up which she was carried to her suite of rooms.

7 April 1900. The Queen with two of her ladies following in a second carriage drove from the Viceregal Lodge to Phoenix Park where 52,000 school-children together with their masters and mistresses had assembled, from all parts of Ireland.

The Queen took a twenty mile drive on most afternoons with a posse round her carriage composed of six constables, two equerries, two grooms and an outrider. As some of the riders became 'saddle-sore' with the continual jog-trotting speed at which the drives were conducted there was some exchanging of the participants and the ranks of the riders became somewhat depleted.

Mid-way through the visit, escorted by the 2nd Life Guards the Queen and her attendants drove to the Adelaide Hospital in a poor part of Dublin where she was greeted by Lord Denbigh, and presented to the Committee of Management, the doctors and the Lady Superintendent - there is no mention of the Queen meeting any of the patients, but she did go on to the Convent of the Sacred Heart, where Lord Denbigh (whom the Queen had especially asked to be present as he was a Catholic) presented her to the Rev Mother Stuart, (Superior Vicar of the Houses) and other clerical dignitaries. Convent pupils and about fifty nuns were also present.

19 April 1900. The Queen was visited by 'all my Jubilee Nurses' from various parts of Ireland assembled on the terrace in front of the Viceregal Lodge, in the afternoon there was a drive along the seashore to Clontarf and a brief call at the house of Lord and Lady Ardilaun, the latter lady presenting Her Majesty with a large 'nosegay' of primroses, it being "Primrose Day".

The following morning there was a visit to the Zoological Gardens, the Queen being very impressed by the lions which she described as "a great feature". In the afternoon - unescorted - there was a drive to meet Lord Denbigh again, this time at the Meath Hospital where the usual presentations of officials took place and then followed a visit to the Convent of Loretto, where 200 nuns and 600 pupils were assembled.

Queen Victoria thoroughly enjoyed her holiday and the party had their photograph taken at the Lodge by Lafayette on Saturday 21st April, afterwards driving through cheering crowds to the Fifteen Acres Review Ground, where the Queen received the royal salute. The Queen then drove in her carriage down the assembled lines and then returned to the saluting point for a march past of first the Naval Brigade, followed by the Field Batteries and Bluejackets, then the Marines, and Troops with small boys from the Hibernian School bringing up the rear.

On Thursday 26 April 1900 the morning of her departure before embarking for Holyhead the Queen gave £1,000 for the Dublin poor, promised a silver cup to the Corporation and aboard the Victoria and Albert II presented Victorian Order medals to twenty-six policemen who had ridden beside her carriage. Others who had accompanied her received souvenirs. Unlike the outward voyage the Irish Sea was in a good mood, the sea calm, the sun shining and as the paddle steamer *Victoria and Albert II* 'flip-flopped' her way back to Holyhead the Queen was able to retire to her quarters and descend into a blissful sleep after the excitements of what was to be her last visit to Ireland.

Whilst the Queen slept peacefully during the crossing there was great activity at Holyhead as the Royal train was prepared for the Queen's return journey and our superb documentary photographer had been busily engaged in making an exhaustive record of events in and around Holyhead, its harbour and railway installations.

Lodge Gates, Viceregal Lodge, Phoenix Park Dublin. 1999. Now the President's Palace, the lodge built in the 1700's by the Duke of Cavendish was the centre-piece of a 1700 acre deer park.   *Carolyn Carr*

Main Entrance, Viceregal Lodge, Phoenix Park Dublin. 1999. *Carolyn Carr*

Viceregal Lodge, Dublin: Queen Victoria is seen with her charming little donkey friend outside the front door of the lodge on the occasion of her visit to Ireland. Now (2001) used as the Irish President's Palace, the lodge, which has been extended over the years, was built in the 1700's by the Duke of Cavendish as a 1700 acre walled park, to be densely inhabited by deer. In David Duff's delightful book "Victoria Travels" is a sympathetic account of Queen Victoria whilst holidaying in Aix-les-Bains, buying a small, thin and weary donkey from a peasant who had it harnessed to a cart. Nursed back to full health and named Jacquot he became a honoured member of the Queen's circle, drawing her small carriage at a gentle pace whilst her courtiers walked alongside chatting to her Majesty. At the end of the holiday Jacquot returned to Windsor with the Queen. History does not so far as we can trace relate whether this is the same little donkey but the delightful story does emphasise Her Majesty's kind heart and regard for all her subjects, equine as well as human.
Christopher Hibbert

Holyhead. April 1900: The square backing on the TALBOT TEM-PERANCE HOTEL, is decorated with flags and bunting as the men of The Welsh Regiment are assembled and inspected. This period picture is in monochrome, but the men of this Volunteer Battalion would have made a colourful display with their red jackets and blue/black trousers with a red stripe down the leg. The white cuffs indicate that these men are most likely The Welsh Regiment (spelling of 'Welsh' changed to 'Welch' in 1920). The regiment today is known as 'The Royal Regiment of Wales (24th/41st Foot). An interesting and unusual feature is the white item tucked into their belts at the back and this looks like a pouch from Slade Wallace equipment worn on the back of the belt (non-regulation). The name comes from Colonel Slade of the Rifle Brigade and Lieutenant Colonel Wallace of the King's Royal Rifles, who introduced an improved design of the equipment 'Valise' in 1888.

Military details *courtesy Malcolm Greensmith - Gemini Prints.*

Queen Victoria sailed back to Holyhead on 26 April 1900. A guard of honour possibly from The Welsh Regiment, denoted by their white cuffs) are closely scrutinised by their Staff Sergeant. The shoulder titles clearly displayed on the sergeant's uniform indicate that they are most likely a Volunteer Battalion, which became known as Territorials in 1902. In 1900 shoulder titles were embroidered (white) but by 1908 metal titles were being worn. In the field the white Slade-Wallace harness, pouches and haversack were stained (sometimes with tea) to a neutral shade. A great advantage of this equipment was that the reduced size valise could speedily be removed and replaced by the haversack, waterproof sheet or blanket. The Union Badge, is the oldest badge of The Welch Regiment and was authorised to be borne on the Colours of the 41st or Invalids Regiment in November 1747. Except for the period 1787 - 1826 the badge was borne continuously by the 41st and its successor the 1st Battalion, The Welch Regiment. It was used as a Regimental crest only and never worn on the uniform dress of the Regiment.

Military details *courtesy Malcolm Greensmith - Gemini Prints*

Holyhead. Station Approach. 26 April 1900: From a vantage point, of one of the windows of the Station Hotel, comes this 'Lowry' style photograph of the guard of honour, complete with their band and enthusiastic accompanying crowds, headed by schoolboys in their 'Sunday best' marching towards the harbour to greet their monarch on her return from Dublin. There is also a splendid view of the station's environs, overbridge, sidings, signalling and standing carriages. The Chester and Holyhead Railway was incorporated on 4 July 1844 to build a 84³/4 mile line between those loca-tions, along the southern shore of the River Dee estuary and the coast of North Wales, proceeding via Abergele and Bangor, thence crossing the Menai Straits by what would be Robert Stephenson's 105 ft high Britannia Tubular Bridge and then traversing the Isle of Anglesey to the growing town and port of Holyhead. A prominent feature towering above the car-riage stock to the left of the picture is the Hydraulic Tower or Accumulator House, which supplied the power to drive the hydraulic cranes and cap-stans situated around the port complex.

Holyhead Station Approach. 26 April 1900: The band marches away from the troops, who are now being marshalled in the roadway, the pavements densely packed with the folk who have accompanied the soldiers from the parade ground. The line was opened from Chester to Saltney Junction (2 miles) on 4 November 1846. Saltney Junction to Bangor was opened 1 May 1848 and from Llanfair to Holyhead on 1 August 1848; prior to the opening of this section passengers for Holyhead were transported by road between Llanfair and Bangor over Telford's suspension bridge until the Britannia Bridge was completed on 18 March 1850. The Government and Admiralty commissions looking into the matter of communications with Ireland had supported the formation of the Chester & Holyhead Railway, although when the railway was incorporated the route for official mail was from London by rail to Liverpool and from that port by steamer to Dublin, this was then the quickest route. The Chester & Holyhead Railway amalgamated with the Mold Railway in 1849 and was worked by the London & North Western Railway from 1856, being vested in that company by an Act of 1858, officially adopted in March of the following year.

Harbour of Refuge. Holyhead. April 1900: The royal yacht *Victoria and Albert II* in whose design the Prince Consort had a hand, displays something of the lines of a sailing ship with her counter stern, graceful bow with tapering bowsprit and pseudo schooner rig. We observe a plentitude of small deck-houses and companionways and in the tradition of paddle-steamer operation the Officer-of-the-Day and his sideman watch events from the starboard-hand paddle-box. When the Sovereign was aboard the following ensigns *(colours worn chiefly by ships)* were displayed. The Admiralty flag is worn at the fore masthead, to denote that the Sovereign is the source from which the powers of the Board of Admiralty are derived, the Royal standard is hoisted at the head of the mainmast and the Union flag *(not Union Jack)* at the mizzen masthead. The Union flag also flies right for'd in our picture and the White ensign is at the stern.

Holyhead Harbour. April 1900: This fascinating picture was taken at low water - note the tide-gauge extreme left-of a delightful steam pinnace laden with elaborately uniformed and cockaded officers and top-hatted dignitaries who have essayed the slippery passage down the steep steps cut into the quay wall to embark and are presumably about to be ferried to audience with Queen Victoria aboard the royal yacht. Note the 'non-nautical' terminology of the notice also left "NO BOAT TO BE LEFT HERE" There is an excellent view of the machinery and boiler, obviously with a good head of steam built up and from the casual attitude of the boatmen, particularly the one pushing the stern away from the quay wall, and the 'unshipped' jack lying across the after thwarts this is a harbour launch and not a naval pinnace.

Holyhead 1900: On this auspicious day at Holyhead, the air was alive with anticipation nowhere more so than on the platforms where the locomotives involved in working the royal train were immaculate in their inimitable livery of 'blackberry black'. Family records indicate that Ben Robinson, of 'Races to the North' fame was probably involved in these royal train workings, but he was not around when these pictures were taken, the train crew being unidentified at the moment. No **291** *Prince of Wales* was the 'pilot engine' as indicated by the single headlamp carried at the top of the smoke box, and would run five minutes ahead of the royal train proper. No 291 owed it's ancestry to Engineer John Ramsbottom, who was appointed to take charge

of the Crewe Works in August 1857. His second locomotive design was the celebrated but perhaps slightly oddly named 'Problem' class of 7ft 6ins 'single driver' express passenger engines, later and more euphoniously known as the 'Lady of the Lake' class. Sixty of these machines were built at Crewe from 1859 to 1865, but they were not numbered consecutively. F. W. Webb rebuilt the entire class from February 1895 onwards, and it is as a 'Webb' rebuild that No 291 appears in this scene, with 16in diameter by 24in stroke cylinders, 7ft 9in driving wheels and an adhesive weight raised from 11$\frac{1}{2}$ tons to 14$\frac{1}{4}$ tons; boiler pressure was 150 lbs per sq in, the grate area was 71 sq ft and the total weight of the engine in working order was 31$\frac{1}{2}$ tons.

Holyhead. April 1900: Buffered up to No. **291** was the royal train engine No. **1915** *Implacable*. Mr F. W. Webb's renowned 'compound' era was now well advanced and No.1915 was a member of the 'Jubilee' class of 4-4-0 four-cylinder compounds which the authority on train running, Rous-Marten concluded after several runs in 1901 were "................capable and successful engines". Construction of this class of locomotive began in earnest in the spring of 1899; eighteen of the class were assembled between March and August 1899, with a further 20 in 1900, and indicative of the 'Royal' interest in maritime matters most of them carried the names of ships of the Royal Navy. Similarly to the pilot-engine No.1915 appears in superb condition, her 'blackberry black' livery glistening and all steel parts burnished to appear like silver. A less well known feature of royal train engines is to be observed behind the open lid of the tool box on the tender. This is the front of the small cab wherein for the length of the journey sat the official appointed to look to the rear watch closely the progression of the following carriages and draw the attention of the engine crew to any signals made by the officials on the train or any mishap to or possible problem with the running of the train.

Harbour of Refuge. Holyhead. April 1900: A 'protected cruiser' of a class of four ships embracing the *Colossus*, and *Edinburgh*, *Ajax* and *Agamemnon*, was in attendance and the naval vessel made a fine sight with flags and pennants displayed. Displaying flags is one of the oldest naval customs. Until 1889 it was left to the junior captain of a fleet or squadron to draw up the order of flags to be worn when ships dressed overall, but full instructions are nowadays specified. The Admiralty's Chief Constructor, Edward Reed, placed the turrets of his earlier Cyclops class warships at either end of a central armoured breastwork. An outmoded concept was the armoured 'fighting top' bristling with light guns to 'rake enemy decks' as in the days of sail.

Note the flexible trunking of the engine and stoke-hold ventilators abaft the bridge and funnel; another hazard with this class of ship with central boilers and engines was working the ammunition stored aft forward to the gun positions.. The boom and suspended mooring lines projecting 'midships, were to accommodate visiting steam picket boats or pinnaces on postal or other harbour duties. These 'protected' cruisers were designed to mount four muzzle loading guns, but a design for a new breech loading 12 inch gun was approved in 1882 and these, following a recommendation by the Controller of the Navy were fitted, together with two 14 inch torpedo tubes. The design of these vessels was deemed a success although the top speed was only 16 knots.

BANGOR

Bangor Station. The official photographer took this shot *(necessarily with a very slow shutter speed)* of Tony (A.J.) Robinson's grandfather John, Assistant Chief Electrical Engineer to the 'Premier Line' The photograph on Page 23 is a companion picture to this, the cameraman having crossed to the opposite side of the carriage for his shot. Bangor Station, by Francis Thompson was a long building with a hipped roof, small partitions at each end supported full length canopies, and additional iron brackets helped to support the weight. For two years whilst the Britannia Bridge was being constructed, Bangor was the temporary terminus of the Chester & Holyhead Railway.

At the time of Queen Victoria's visit to Holyhead, Bangor Cathedral was greatly admired, and had been partly restored in 1868 - 70 by G. G. Scott and in 1880 by J. O. Scott. Another handsome building was Lloyds Bank in the High Street, built in 1887 in the Elizabethan style with a fine Clock Tower. The famous University founded in 1884 featured impressive quadrangular buildings; a Teacher Training College was established c.1860. Just east of the town was the Pennant family's neo-Norman style Penrhyn Castle, the Lords Penrhyn owning the quarries at Bethesda and having their own outlet to the sea for the slate at Port Penrhyn.

Bangor Station. April 1900: A definitive shot *(including the 'ducket' and outside communication cord at roof level)* taken from the opposite side of the carriage to that on the preceding page. The running on board of the island platform *(right)* reads " BANGOR- Change here for - BETHESDA, CAERNARVON, and LLANBERIS" and the signals on the gantry beyond the No.1 Signal Box at the tunnel mouth read, on the approach side : left to right - Down Goods Loop, Down Pass. Loop, Bethesda Branch, Down Main. (Bethesda was closed to passengers 3rd December 1951 and entirely 7 October 1963). Following several accidents at the sleeper crossing in the foreground,

this was replaced by a subway in 1924 when the station was rebuilt, and the signal box was replaced, a location for the new and larger cabin being excavated in the cliff face. Note 'Anglicised' spelling of names. Space was always at a premium at Bangor, the station being perforce restricted to the short site between Bangor Tunnel (East) and Belmont Tunnel (West). Within these constrictions room was found for the passenger and freight stations, and associated track-work, the Motive Power Department and Civil Engineer's Department. Constant modifications and improvements to the layout began in 1852 and continued over the years.

Also lying nearby was this elegant naval screw steamer, with graceful bowsprit, delightful sheer line and counter stern, with steam pinnace alongside. As evidence of its official identity the steamer wears the Union Flag *(which is not allowed to be worn by other than naval vessels)* at the jack, with the White Ensign at the foremast and the red St George's Cross on a white ground flag of an 'Admiral of the Main'. From early in the 17th century the fleets of the Royal Navy were divided into Red, White and Blue Squadrons, and later each squadron was distinguished by wearing Red, White and Blue ensigns respectively. This system was discontinued by Parliamentary Acts of 1864 and 1865 and the White Ensign was authorised to be worn by all ships of the Royal Navy. The Blue Ensign was allocated to ships belonging to public offices and colonial navies and the Red Ensign assigned to the Merchant Navy who, in any event had used it as their colours since 1700.

April 1900: Also lying in the harbour and splendidly dressed for the Royal event was the Liverpool Pilot Boat No.4 *David Fernie.* The Liverpool Pilot Service was established on a formal basis in 1776 but their pilot boats were sailing vessels until 1896, when the first of a class of four steam cutters, No.1 *Francis Henderson* was built by Murdock & Murray at Port Glasgow. No.2 *Leonard Spear* followed in the same year and in 1898 came No. 3 *Queen Victoria* and No.4 *David Fernie.* The four steamers were all of 275 grt, 128ft 2ins length x 24ft 1in beam x 11ft 7ins depth. No.4 was sold out of service in 1937 to interests in Oslo. The end of the long established four cutter, sea keeping pilot service came in December 1962 when the 579 grt steam cutter *William M. Clarke of 1937* was de-commissioned. The shore-based pilots are now taken out from Liverpool and Point Lynas to their stations by fast motor launches.

Holyhead. April 1900: The royal yacht *Victoria & Albert II* lies at her berth beside the Admiralty Pier and the group of sailors for'd of the bridge will be discussing the final arrangements for mooring the vessel securely and positioning her exactly abreast of the point where Her Majesty Queen Victoria will disembark to be greeted by the assembled dignitaries and her Guard of Honour. Interesting nautical features are the yacht's dummy open gun ports, the diversity of small clerestories on the deck which would give light to the saloons on the main deck below, and the corresponding pletho-ra of companionways. One service gangway leading from ship to shore, already extended is observed on the extreme left close to the starb'd paddle box; secured to a single davit is a gangway which would be used by vessels coming alongside to discharge goods or passengers when the vessel was out in the stream. A very elegant pulling 'gig' is observed beneath davits to the right of the picture. Between the graceful bell-mouthed funnels and on the navigating bridge which spans the paddle-boxes is located the steering position displaying a massive triple wheeled helm.

Holyhead. The royal yacht *Victoria and Albert II* is now berthed alongside the Admiralty (Mail) Pier, 'starboard side to' but the 'brow', the 'Navy' term for the gangway connecting the ship to the wharf has not yet been secured and the guard of honour mounted by Rifle Volunteers of 2 Welsh Battalion lending colour to the scene with their red jackets and blue/black uniform trousers, with a red stripe, are 'standing easy' whilst all is made fast. It is possible to distinguish the 'Austrian Knot' on the sleeves and possibly green facings also. The 'Austrian Knot' in its simple form was often called the 'Crows Foot' or 'Clover Leaf'. This special knot was worn in braid on the sleeves of tunics not only of Austrian troops but in the late 19th century by the British Army also. The gangway will span the gap between the royal yacht and the quay below the spot where two officers are noted watching events from their position on the starboard-hand paddle-box. Below decks Queen Victoria will be taking her place in her wheelchair assisted by her Indian servant and ladies in waiting and will then be wheeled across the narrow gap between ship and shore, at a point indicated by the launch suspended from davits *(centre)*. The open dummy gun ports at main deck level are also a feature of this picture.

Military Details. ***Malcolm Greensmith - Gemini Prints***

Holyhead, April 1900: Attended by one of her Indian servants and two Ladies in Waiting, Queen Victoria seated in her wheel-chair is being pushed towards the 'brow' which will give her access from the royal yacht to the Quayside where the guard mounted by Rifle Volunteers of 2 Welsh Battalion in their colourful uniforms are waiting to greet her as of course are local dignitaries and officials. Pictures of the Queen in her wheelchair are sparse as Her Majesty preferred not to be seen 'wheeled around' in public. Although we now know that she was nearing the end of her reign as monarch for almost 64 years she was considering plans for her holidays in the year 1901, having come through the period of intense melancholy and mourning that followed the death of the Prince Consort in 1861 from typhoid, at the early age of 42 years. In those desperately sad days following Albert's death she was supported by the devotion of the Scottish servant John Brown, who until his death in March 1883 had stood at her right-hand for over two decades. As a token of her high regard for the gruff old Highlander Queen Victoria dedicat

ed to him her charming book *"More Leaves from the Journal of a Life in the Highlands 1862 - 1882."* A statue to John Brown was erected at Balmoral. In these latter years Queen Victoria was intensely interested in the British Empire, and particularly Indian affairs following her appointment as Empress of India on May Day 1876. A banqueting hall in the Indian fashion known as the Durbar Room was constructed at Osborne House. In August 1889 when Queen Victoria went to stay for a few days with Sir Henry Robertson at Pale Hall, in Merioneth, North Wales, her Indian servants were an indispensable part of the retinue and she was accompanied by no less than six of these personages who appeared as an amazing and colourful spectacle in their brilliant satins and turbans to the local people. In this same year Abdul Karim was appointed as the Queen's 'Munshi' that is her secretary or clerk; one of his duties in this post was to instruct Her Majesty in the Hindustani language. Osborne House and some of the Royal apartments are open to the public on certain days.

Holyhead. 26 April 1900: In the preceding pictures we viewed the berthing of the royal yacht *Victoria and Albert II,* setting up of the gangways between ship and pier, and the opening stages of Queen Victoria's disembarkation. In his inimitable style our photographer Mr Banks has captured the moment when Her Majesty having 'come ashore' passed through the throng awaiting her and beneath the scroll of welcome which may be seen suspended from the valance of the platform awning just above the centre of the picture. We have another excellent view of the guard of honour mounted by Rifle Volunteers of 2 Welsh Battalion. They are 'presenting arms' and one can only reiterate what a fine and colourful sight they must have exhibited with their smart red tunics and blue/black, red striped trousers, smart helmets and polished accoutrements. This picture also enables us to see something of the general public gathered on the pier and platforms behind the soldiery to greet the Queen. Although one or two top hats can be seen most of the gentlemen seem to have removed their head-gear in deference to the occasion as one would have expected. Some of the ladies on the extreme right of the gathering are wearing 'sailor collars' and 'navy style' straw hats. Beneath the awning are draped festoons of laurel leaves and we know from the picture on page No. 4 *(bottom)* that the interior of the station was similarly adorned.

Holyhead. Tuesday March 20 1900: Presaging the return visit by Queen Victoria from her last journey to Ireland, the royal train is seen at Holyhead. In the picture *(extreme right)* is a party of railway officials, the covered van behind the 'brake' conveyed the Queen's carriage or landau. The train engine was a four cylinder compound 4-4-0 of the Jubilee class, the first of the compound engines to have coupled driving wheels. In the main these engines were named after contemporary warships No **1915** being named *Implacable*. HSH Prince Louis of Battenberg took command of the battleship *Implacable* in 1901 but before that was present at Queen Victoria's funeral. When the horses waiting to draw the gun carriage which was to carry the coffin became very restive he suggested that sailors who were forming a guard of honour should draw the gun-carriage instead. This custom has since been followed at all royal funerals and those of high-ranking naval officers. The L&NWR signals are also an interesting feature in their own right. On 13 June 1842, a little less than six decades before her last Irish visit, Queen Victoria made her first railway journey and although many people still regarded rail travel as hazardous, the example of their Queen lent an aura of respectability to this new mode of travel which would stand the embryo rail promoters in good stead. Not that Queen Victoria was not apprehensive in the first instance, but doubtless she would have been encouraged and supported by her beloved Prince Albert who was always receptive to new ideas. The Royal Saloon which the Queen was to use had been built 'on spec' as it were by David Davies, a London coachbuilder, to the order of the Great Western Railway before this undertaking was proposed. The journey was to be from Slough to Paddington, and the train comprised a second-class brake carriage, two posting carriages for the suite, and three carriage trucks to carry the royal equipages. The engine was one of Gooch's seven foot singles named *Plegethon* and it was driven by no less a personage than Locomotive Superintendent Daniel Gooch himself, accompanied on the engine by Mr I. K. Brunel. At 12 noon Queen Victoria, Prince Albert and all the royal party were aboard the train and everyone arrived safely at Paddington old station just twenty-five minutes later.

National Railway Museum

Crewe. Friday 27 April 1900 1.33pm Back to Windsor: Queen Victoria's royal train, but this time without the inclusion of the carriage truck behind the leading brake, is seen on the curve at Crewe. Compound 4-4-0 No **1915** *Implacable* still in charge. Observe on the tender, the rear facing cab for the man whose duty it was to keep a constant watch on the following carriages and transmit to the driver any signals made by the officials travelling with the royal party. The train was booked to depart from Holyhead (Pier Head) at 11. 0am, and Llandudno Junction at 11.58 am, Chester, arrive 12.55am depart 1.5pm, and as in our picture Crewe 106½ miles at 1.33pm. The journey continued via Wolverhampton, Birmingham, Oxford and Slough (West Curve) 5.24pm to arrive at Windsor 271¼ miles at 5.30pm. *National Railway Museum*

Holyhead. Inner Harbour. April 1900: Top hats and Inchcape cloaks set the scene, in the forefront a very prosperous looking gentleman paces with his hands clasped behind his back. To his right is the obelisk and clock tower which commemorated the official opening of the Holyhead New Harbour, Station and Hotel on Thursday, 17 June 1880, by HRH The Prince of Wales, later King Edward VII. The signpost pointing to the left of the indicator clock reads "ORDINARY TRAINS FOR CHESTER" that on the right declaims "NEXT TRAIN WILL DEPART" whilst that pointing forwards out of the picture indicates that the top-hatted gentleman may have come from the "IRISH MAIL BOAT". Whilst they were in the process of completing the new station and hotel the L&NWR took over a local hostelry, the Eagle & Child and operated it for the benefit of their passengers under the name of The Royal Hotel.

Holyhead. 5 August 1995: A present day view of the station approach graced with the obelisk featured above by the Inner Harbour at the turn of the century. Now, to commemorate the opening of the 'New Port of Holyhead' on 10 July 1995 last the handsomely ornate obelisk cum clock tower, with its splendid dado, scroll work, abacus, frieze, cornice and pediment, indeed a plethora of architectural paraphernalia, has been moved from its position at the Inner Harbour, to this position at the head of the station approach. The clock tower of course, when first commissioned commemorated the opening of the 1880 harbour by the Prince of Wales. A more modern approach to such occasions is signified by the tasteful circular plaque wall-mounted inside the enclosed, main circulation area or concourse, the windows of which look out upon the Inner Harbour. This states in the Welsh and English tongues that it is "To commemorate the official opening of the new port of Holyhead 10 July 1995 by Rachel Hughes age 9 and Paul Ryan age 9.

A J Robinson

"THE ONLY WAY TO TRAVEL" London & North Western Railway Paddle and Screw Steamers berthed at Holyhead dressed overall in honour of Queen Victoria's passage through the port on her return to this country on the 26th April 1900 from her visit to Ireland. At the outset the funnel colours of the railway steamers were white with a black top, but this was soon changed to the better known buff with black top. Later steamers had cowled (or 'Navy top') funnels whilst retaining the buff and black livery. The L&NWR house flag was a red pennant, carrying a white St George's Cross, inset with a circle carrying the well known Britannia arms of the company. On the extreme left is the frame of one of the hydraulic cranes which were such a prominent feature of the loading/unloading berths.

In our upper picture, the leading personage striding out vigorously ahead of this group of four important looking gentlemen, thought to be L&NWR officials, are hurrying towards one of the 'Premier Line's' latest screw steamers where in subsequent scenes we shall see the vessel's Master entertaining them to what was no doubt a sumptuous lunch. It might be safely assumed that this was on April 26th after Queen Victoria had been safely disembarked from the royal yacht and the general air of tension and excitement engendered by the great occasion was winding down. An interesting feature of platform furniture is the 'rolling gate' for crowd control to the right of the picture.

HOLYHEAD STATION

- A - CENTURY BETWEEN

Holyhead. Saturday 5 August 1995: The rolling stock and ancillary buildings denote the passing of the years, but although the locations are not exactly duplicated the basic structural features of this part of the station buildings, e.g. the walls with their fenestrated arches, oversailing courses or corbels and buttresses had, when this photograph was taken stood the passage of time comparatively unaltered unashamed of their Victorian heritage. *A J Robinson*

Holyhead Harbour. 26 April 1900: A group of officials invited to lunch with the vessel's master go aboard a London & North Western Railway steamer, dressed overall in honour of Queen Victoria's visit lying alongside the Departure Berth in the Inner Harbour.

HOLYHEAD HARBOUR

Holyhead. Passenger departure berth. April 1900: In the normal course of embarkation it was only necessary for travellers arriving by train to join the steamers to walk across the platform to reach their boat. In this instance however the group of gentleman making their way up the gangway and coming aboard are, it is thought being conducted to the saloon. There had been some consternation in London & North Western Railway circles when in 1896 the City of Dublin Steam Packet Co., the Government Contractors for the Royal Mail put their new 24 knot T.S.S. *Ulster II*, the first of a quartet of such steamers on their Holyhead - Kingstown station, at a time when the crack vessel of the L&NWR fleet was the oddly named P.S. *Banshee*, built by Laird Brothers at Birkenhead in 1884, although a fine steamer in her time this 1,109 g.t. 310 ft long paddler, fitted with 2 cylinder, oscillating engines of 3,000 i.h.p. was by now somewhat outdated and old fashioned.

To Promenade Deck

1st Class Smoking Room

1st Class Saloon

Waiting for lunch ! : The L&NWR responded to the challenge of the City of Dublin company by commissioning on 15 December 1897 the first of their own quartet of twin-screw steamers from Denny & Co., the 1842 g. t. *Cambria III*, fitted with two twin sets of high speed Triple-expansion reciprocating engines. The design speed for *Cambria* and her sisters was 21 knots and as the Holyhead - North Wall, passage was longer than that of the rival mail boat run to Kingstown, and high speed runs up the River Liffey not countenanced there was no question of out and out racing between the steamers. In our picture above the party has been joined by the vessel's Master *(three pips and a gold band, Merchant Navy uniforms were not formalised at this time)*. Since 1850 it had been a requirement that company Deck Officers had certificates of competency, and when our picture was taken officers had to hold 'foreign going' rather than merely 'home trade' qualifications. Promotion was by seniority, working up through the ranks from the cargo boats to the passenger steamers. *Cambria III* was renamed *Arvonia* when her name was needed for a new turbine steamer which replaced her in 1920. She passed to the L&MSR at the grouping, worked on the Isle of Man and Greenore sailings and was scrapped in August 1925. Note the signs in the deck-head directing passengers to the PROMENADE DECK, 1ST CLASS SMOKING ROOM AND 1ST CLASS SALOON respectively.

Holyhead "The Captain's Table. April 1900: The master of a L&NWR steamer, probably of the 'Cambria' class of 1897 entertains guests, in the saloon with non-alcoholic beverages judging by the tableware. An interesting sidelight on human nature is that of the gentleman on the extreme right furtively finishing his meal whilst his companions pose for their photograph. Close examination of this detailed picture and crisp scene reveals the London & North Western Railway Company's 'Britannia' emblem emblazoned on the chair backs, chairs were often chained to the deck to prevent their gyrating in bad weather. Note the fine sideboard, left, with a splendid display of decanters and glassware, and equipped with 'fiddles' to retain the tableware when the ship rolled. The deck is covered with handsome carpeting to company design.. A fine 'stand-by' oil lamp (as electric lighting was installed) rests in gimbals secured to the magnif-icently panelled bulkhead, and for ventilation whilst alongside the circular ports *(right)* are clipped up in the open position. The 'halation' effect round the port-holes indicates that the picture was a time exposure made using available light. It is worth recalling that in common with the Isle of Man boats the Holyhead steamers sailed whatever the conditions, unlike today's highly sophisticated vessels where sailings may be cancelled if sea and wind conditions reach pre-determined levels. Until 1894 when the Company took over the service it was customary in Maritime circles for the Captain and Steward to run the catering services very much for their own benefit. When the L&NWR's Masters lost this additional source of income, those men long established with the company received an additional 'allowance' to their pay as compensation for the rest of the time they remained with the company.

Holyhead. April 1900: The square does not look its best in this picture depicting a series of rather dilapidated buildings, with the Kings Arms left, perhaps catering for seamen and commercial travellers mainly. and the Marine Hotel left of centre, There is a typical eating house of the period right centre and the solitary uniformed figure probably a railwayman or seaman.

HOLYHEAD

THEN
&
NOW

(Right) Holyhead. Saturday 5 August 1995. There has been some demolition of property in the square, but even so, despite the parked cars, and some modernisation of other buildings, Tony Robinson had no difficulty in recognising the location of the scene that Mr Banks photographed so many decades ago. Tony visited the port to capture on film some of the contrasts that almost a century had brought to the locality. To quantify the situation, the Kings Arms stood as foursquare and ready to cater for the thirsty traveller in 1995 as it had in Queen Victoria's day.

A J Robinson

Holyhead. Inner Harbour April 1900: The photographer's stance was backing the Clock Tower and Monument, seen in previous pictures, and shows the Passenger Departure Berth left, and Passenger Arrival Berth right. The red ensign displayed at the stern of one of the lovely old L&NWR paddle steamers possible the PS *Violet* or another of her class reminds us of the days when the British Mercantile Marine was one of the most important fleets in the world. A coaling barge can be discerned discharging 'bunkers' to a steamer berthed on the right. The goods shed and cattle landings are adjacent to the towering set of sheerlegs dimly seen in the haze left of centre and when a red light was hoisted at this point vessels were not permitted to enter the inner harbour. Also faint outlines in the far distance beyond the harbour entrance are the buildings of the Custom House and Harbour Office on the Admiralty Pier.

(Right) Holyhead Inner Harbour. Reconstruction Work Saturday 5 August 1995: By this time some £42m had been invested in redesigning and reconstructing the port of Holyhead. Special linkspans to accommodate the HSS (High Speed Service) craft were towed from Finland to the port. The new linkspan seen under construction here weighed 600 tonnes and is 37m wide, of five vehicle lane ramp capacity it was anticipated that putting the new structure in place would take about ten days. Provision is for the HSS craft to be unloaded via the stern doors, and the centre lane of the five lane ramp was intended to load ships stores in specially designed containers. The structure was also fitted with equipment for guiding the vessel into her berth and taking on and replenishing her stocks of oil fuel and water during the scheduled 30 minute turn round.   *A J Robinson*

Holyhead Station. April 1900: At the turn of the century one of the important projects supervised by the London & North Western Railway's Assistant Chief Electrical Engineer, with special responsibility for all Non-Traction Activities, John Robinson, based first at Crewe and later Euston, was to implement the transition from gas to electric lighting of the 'Premier Line's' most important stations, particularly Holyhead, in view of Queen Victoria's impending visit. Hence his invitation, by right, to be present at this prestigious Royal function. In marked contrast to the three pendant gas lamps one of the new electric lighting fittings appears in the picture and close scrutiny also shows the 'bus lines' carrying the power to the fittings. And what a wonderful example of Victorian railway travel is captured here. John Robinson himself is thought to be the bowler hatted gentleman looking forward from the open carriage window beneath the 'Harrison' communication cord. Another similarly clad gentleman close to the platform trolley looks rather sternly towards the cameraman, who must be struggling with a massive tripod-mounted camera, focussing an 'upside down image' on a dim ground-glass screen. Perhaps the policeman with his back to the lens is there to keep a clear space, and other constabulary helmets can be discerned in the press of folk. Is the attractive young lady just to the right of the scene, a domestic servant hurrying back to her place of service following her 'afternoon off'? How many of these ordinary folk we might speculate, frozen for a moment of eternity on the glass plate lived, through the Edwardian era and the horrors of the Kaiser's War to see the dawn of the Roaring Twenties?

Holyhead. Admiralty Pier: Although not specifically dated, other than April 1900, since the pictures in the 'Robinson Family album' seem to follow in a logical sequence it also seems logical to assume that, being near the end of the book, this magnificent photograph, redolent with period atmosphere and unlike some of the other scenes taken in brilliant sunshine, was perhaps taken when Queen Victoria's disembarkation was complete and the overcast skies had cleared along with the departing crowds. The scene is undoubtedly worthy of a place in this collection, with it's charming pastiche of the old lady and young girl, surely grandma and grand-daughter. It is worth bearing in mind that although to our present-day eyes 'grandma' would seem to be aged in the 80's she was probably not much over 60 years of age, if that! A seaman can be seen 'on watch' on the open bridge of the paddle steamer beside the steering wheel and engine room telegraph. Luggage seems to be assembled ready to go aboard and to the right of the lad porter and his more senior colleague seen left of centre is a miscellaneous pile of luggage on a trolley. To the left of the pair is the entrance to the train platform.

Holyhead. Admiralty Pier: The young lady and her grandmother (Page 41) were probably waiting for the luggage to be loaded onto the paddle steamer portrayed in this scene. From the steep slope of the gangways it obviously very near to low water, the elderly sailor coming up the right-hand slope seems to be having some difficulty in ascending, whilst a colleague is steadying the huge basket which another porter is essaying to carry down the other precipitous gangway. When loads such as this were manhandled regularly as part of the daily round it is little wonder that the life expectancy of a working man was so much shorter a century ago than is the case today. Holyhead Harbours were sheltered by a breakwater, composed chiefly of rubble which extended about 1¹/2 miles east - north - eastward, in a double curve, from Soldiers Point, situated about 1¹/4 miles eastward of North Stack. Lat 53 19" N., Long. 4 41' W. The Holyhead Harbour of Refuge occupied the whole space within the breakwater, except Old and Inner Harbours which lie eastward of the town of Holyhead. New Harbour was that part within the breakwater and westward of the Outer Platters. A stone pier known as Admiralty Pier, projects about 2 cables eastward from the southern end of Ynys Halen, the space southward of this pier known as Old Harbour. Inner Harbour which was entered through Old harbour was an artificial harbour formed by dredging and land reclamation. The character of the port of Holyhead and the types of shipping using the facilities are vastly different today to those captured by our photographer so many decades ago.

LATTER - DAY HOLYHEAD

(Above) Holyhead, May 1988: The passage of time has not impacted on the appearance of the Admiralty Pier, the Custom House or in the main the Harbour Office buildings. T. Harrison's Memorial Arch built in 1824 to commemorate the visit of George IV when he took passage from the port in the P.S. *Lightning*, 205 tons commanded by Captain Skinner as recounted on Page 7 still stands proudly at the entrance to the Admiralty Pier. The legend celebrating the erection of the memorial and the royal visit is inscribed above the lintel in Latin on the one side and the Welsh language on the other. The B&I Line's M.V. *Leinster* is seen entering the inner Harbour from Dublin. She was about two hours late due to tidal conditions at Holyhead.

Bottom. In this second scene, taken on the north side of the harbour on the same day and again looking across to the Admiralty Pier, the moveable bridge over the entrance to the dry dock, is a prominent and interesting feature. For obvious security reasons it is securely shackled by chain to the massive bollard (centre) and on the further wall through the protective railings the depth gauge stands out clearly on the further wall of the unoccupied dry dock. Both pictures *Harold D. Bowtell*

- Significant Dates and Events in Queen Victoria's Life and Reign -

24 May 1819	Birth of Victoria
26 Aug 1819	Birth of Albert
20 June 1837	Victoria told of her accession to the throne
28 June 1838	Coronation of Queen Victoria
Oct 1839	Albert visits Windsor Castle
10 Feb 1840	Marriage of Queen Victoria and Prince Albert
10 June 1840	Attempt on Victoria's life (the first of seven such throughout her reign)
21 Nov 1840	Vicky, the first of Victoria and Albert's nine children born
1845	Osborne House on the Isle of Wight purchased
Sep 1848	First visit to Balmoral
1 May 1851	Opening of the Great Exhibition
1854 - 6	Crimean War
1857	Victoria appoints Prince Albert as Consort
14 Dec 1861	Death of Prince Albert
Dec 1864	John Brown brought down to Osborne House
6 Feb 1866	The Queen opens Parliament for the first time since becoming widowed
1868	Publication of the Queen's "Leaves from the Journal of Our Life in the Highlands"

Nov 1871	The Prince of Wales contracts typhoid (the disease responsible for Albert's death)
27 Feb 1872	Prince of Wales recovers. Thanksgiving Service held.
3 July 1872	Albert memorial opened
May Day 1876	Victoria becomes Empress of India
1879	Zulu War
29 Mar 1883	Death of John Brown
21 June 1887	Queen Victoria's Golden Jubilee Thanksgiving Service. National rejoicing
23 June 1887	Abdul Karim (The Munshi) appointed as Queen's servant.
1889	Abdul Karim now becomes the Queen's personal Munshi or Clerk
22 June 1897	Queen Victoria's Diamond Jubilee Procession
11 Oct 1899	'Second' Boer War

3 April 1900	Queen Victoria visits Ireland sailing from Holyhead on the Victoria and Albert.
26 April 1900	Queen Victoria makes the return passage from Dublin to Holyhead aboard the Victoria and Albert

22 Jan 1901	DEATH OF QUEEN VICTORIA AT OSBORNE HOUSE ON THE ISLE OF WIGHT